FOOD LOVERS

GRILLS & SALADS

RECIPES SELECTED BY JONNIE LÉGER

Trans
Atlantic
Press

All recipes serve four people, unless otherwise indicated.

For best results when cooking the recipes in this book, buy fresh ingredients and follow the instructions carefully. Make sure that everything is properly cooked through before serving, particularly any meat and shellfish, and note that as a general rule vulnerable groups such as the very young, elderly people, pregnant women, convalescents and anyone suffering from an illness should avoid dishes that contain raw or lightly cooked eggs.

For all recipes, quantities are given in standard U.S. cups and imperial measures, followed by the metric equivalent. Follow one set or the other, but not a mixture of both because conversions may not be exact. Standard spoon and cup measurements are level and are based on the following:

1 tsp = 5 ml, 1 tbsp = 15 ml, 1 cup = 250 ml / 8 fl oz.

Note that Australian standard tablespoons are 20 ml, so Australian readers should use 3 tsp in place of 1 tbsp when measuring small quantities.

The electric oven temperatures in this book are given for conventional ovens with top and bottom heat. When using a fan oven, the temperature should be decreased by about 20–40°F / 10–20°C – check the oven manufacturer's instruction book for further guidance. The cooking times given should be used as an approximate guideline only.

CONTENTS

BEEF AND VEGETABLE SALAD WITH PEANUTS

Ingredients

500 g /about 1 lb beef sirloin

1 tbsp. oil

8 oz / 250 g carrots, cut into matchsticks

8 oz / 250 g green beans, trimmed

7 oz / 200 g broccoli florets

2 scallions (spring onions), cut into rings

For the dressing:

6 tbsp. lemon juice

6 tbsp. sunflower oil

1 tsp. sesame oil

1 tsp. cane sugar

1 tsp. ginger, finely chopped

1 clove garlic, finely chopped

Salt & freshly ground pepper

In addition:

2/3 cup / 100 g roasted peanuts

1 green chili

Method

Prep and cook time: 50 min

1 Preheat the oven to 325°F (160°C/ Gas Mark 3). Trim the beef. Heat the oil and brown the meat on all sides and then put it into the preheated oven and roast for about 20 minutes. Take out, wrap in aluminum foil and let rest in the oven at a very low heat.

2 Blanch the vegetables (apart from the spring onions) one after the other in boiling, salted water (carrots and broccoli for 4 minutes each, beans for about 8 minutes). When each vegetable has been blanched, take out of the pan, refresh in cold water and drain.

3 For the dressing, mix all the dressing ingredients and season to taste.

4 Mix the prepared salad ingredients with half of the dressing. Trim the chili and cut into thin rings. Slice the beef thinly across the grain and mix lightly with the salad. Arrange on a large platter, sprinkle with the rest of the dressing and scatter with peanuts and chili rings.

SMOKED SALMON AND APPLE SALAD

Ingredients

2 red onions, sliced

2 apples, cored and sliced

4 gherkins, sliced

14 oz / 400 g thinly sliced smoked salmon

2 tbsp pickled green peppercorns

¼ cup oil

½ cup balsamic vinegar

2 tsp honey

Salt and freshly ground pepper, to taste

Method

Prep and cook time: 15 min

1 Gently arrange the sliced onions, apples and gherkins on 4 plates. Lay the smoked salmon slices on top. Sprinkle with peppercorns.

2 In a small bowl, whisk the oil, vinegar and honey to make a vinaigrette; season with salt and pepper and serve with the salad.

CHICKPEA AND SPINACH SALAD

Ingredients

4 tbsp olive oil

2 tbsp cider vinegar

1 tsp medium-hot dry mustard

1 pinch sugar

Salt and freshly ground pepper, to taste

6 cups / 350 g baby spinach leaves

14-oz / 400-g can chickpeas, rinsed and drained

2 beefsteak tomatoes, cored, seeded and diced

1 ripe avocado, pitted and diced

8 plums, pitted and cut into wedges

3 scallions (spring onions), finely chopped

Method

Prep and cook time: 20 min

1 Whisk together the oil, vinegar, mustard and sugar in a large bowl to make a vinaigrette. Season with salt and pepper.

2 Add the spinach, chickpeas, tomatoes, avocado, plums and scallions (spring onions) and toss gently to coat. Divide between four plates and serve.

CHICKEN IN SPICY COCONUT

Ingredients

2 cloves garlic, finely chopped

1 chili, sliced (wear gloves to prevent irritation)

1 tsp freshly grated ginger

1¾ cups / 200 ml coconut milk

Zest and juice of 1 lime

4 chicken breasts, chopped into chunks

Wooden skewers

Sesame oil

Salt & freshly milled pepper

Method

Prep and cook time: 20 min plus Marinating time: 12 h

1 Mix the garlic, ginger, chili, coconut milk, lime juice and zest to make a marinade and then mix with the diced chicken. For the best results put into a plastic bag so that everything is well covered and marinate in the refrigerator overnight.

3 Soak the wooden skewers in enough water to cover for 30 minutes (to prevent burning). Preheat the broiler (grill). Take the chicken out of the marinade, thread onto wooden skewers, sprinkle with a little oil and season with salt and pepper. Grill for 5–6 minutes, or until cooked through, turning occasionally.

SESAME CRUSTED TUNA

Ingredients

1¾ lb / 800 g fresh tuna fillet
(a longish piece)

Salt and freshly ground pepper, to taste

6 tbsp soy sauce, divided

5 oz / 150 g cellophane noodles

1 lb / about 400 g sugar snap peas,
trimmed and halved lengthwise

Juice of 2 limes

1 tbsp fish sauce

1 pinch sugar

1 bunch scallions (spring onions),
thinly sliced along the diagonal

1 bunch cilantro (coriander) leaves,
finely chopped (reserve a few whole
leaves for garnish)

4 hot red chilies, seeded and thinly
sliced (wear gloves to prevent
irritation)

3 tbsp sesame oil

2 tbsp white sesame seeds

2 tbsp black sesame seeds

Method

Prep and cook time: 50 min

1 Season the fish with salt and pepper and sprinkle
with 3 tablespoons of the soy sauce. Cover and
marinate in the refrigerator 30 minutes.

2 Meanwhile, put the cellophane noodles into a
bowl, pour plenty of boiling water over them and let
stand until softened, 10 minutes. Drain and cut into
shorter lengths with kitchen scissors; set aside.

3 Cook the sugar snap peas in boiling salted water
just until bright green, 1-2 minutes; drain in a
colander under cold running water to stop cooking.
Set aside.

4 Whisk the lime juice, the remaining soy sauce,
fish sauce, and sugar in a large bowl; season with
salt and pepper. Add the sugar snap peas, scallions
(spring onions), cilantro (coriander) and chilies and
toss to coat. Add the cellophane noodles and
toss gently.

5 Heat the sesame oil in a wok or large skillet. Pat
the tuna dry with paper towels and sear quickly on
both sides. Roll in sesame seeds and slice thickly.

6 Divide the salad onto plates, add a few slices of
tuna to each and garnish with the reserved cilantro
(coriander) leaves.

BEAN SALAD WITH ONIONS AND TOMATOES

Ingredients

6 tbsp olive oil

½ cup / 100 ml vegetable broth (stock)

4 tbsp white wine vinegar

½ tsp dry mustard

Salt and freshly ground pepper, to taste

1 pint / 500 g cocktail tomatoes, halved

2 cups / 150 g canned small white beans (eg navy or haricot), rinsed and drained

2 red onions, thinly sliced

Fresh parsley leaves, for garnish

Method

Prep and cook time: 30 min

1 In a medium bowl, whisk the oil, broth, vinegar and mustard to make a vinaigrette; season with salt and pepper.

2 Add the tomatoes, beans and onions and toss to coat. Let stand 20 minutes to marinate.

3 Sprinkle a few parsley leaves over the salad before serving.

LAMB AND POTATO SALAD

Ingredients

1¼ lb / 600 g potatoes, peeled and quartered

Salt and freshly ground pepper, to taste

Olive oil

2 red bell peppers, cored and quartered lengthwise

About 1 lb / 500 g loin of lamb, trimmed of fat

1 tsp curry powder

2 tbsp lemon juice

2 tbsp wine vinegar

4 cups / 175 g baby salad greens

8 oz / 200 g mini mozzarella balls

Method

Prep and cook time: 1 hour

1 Season the potatoes with salt and pepper, scatter them in an oven dish and drizzle with a little of the olive oil.

2 Preheat the broiler (grill). Line a broiler pan with foil. Place the bell pepper pieces skin-side-up on the pan and broil (grill) until the skin blisters and blackens. Take out, cover with a damp cloth and let cool. Then skin and cut into strips.

3 Season the lamb with salt and pepper and rub with a tablespoon of the oil. Put under the hot grill for 3–5 minutes each side, depending on preference and the thickness of the meat. Wrap in foil and set aside.

4 Reduce the temperature to 350°F (180°C / Gas Mark 4) and bake the potatoes for 20–25 minutes, turning occasionally.

5 Mix the curry powder with 3 tablespoons of the oil in a small bowl and brush the mixture onto the potatoes. Continue baking for a further 10 minutes, or until tender.

6 In a large bowl, whisk about 4 tablespoons of olive oil, the lemon juice and vinegar to make a vinaigrette. Add the salad greens and gently toss to coat; season with salt and pepper. Divide between 4 bowls and add the mozzarella. Thinly slice the meat and put on top of the salad with the potatoes. Scatter with the pepper strips and serve at once.

ASPARAGUS AND WATERCRESS SALAD

Ingredients

½ lb / 250 g asparagus, trimmed

8 thin slices bacon, halved

4 tbsp olive oil

1-2 tbsp lemon juice

1 tbsp balsamic vinegar

½ tsp sugar

½ tsp medium-hot dry mustard

½ tsp salt

Freshly ground pepper, to taste

1–2 shallots, finely diced

3 cups / 100 g baby spinach leaves, trimmed

2 cups / 100 g watercress, trimmed

2 medium tomatoes, thinly sliced

About 4 oz / 100 g Parmesan cheese

Method

Prep and cook time: 30 min

1 Cook the asparagus in boiling salted water until bright green but still quite al dente, 5 minutes ; drain in a colander under cold running water to stop cooking.

2 Fry the bacon until crisp in a dry nonstick skillet; drain on paper towels.

3 In a large bowl, whisk the oil, lemon juice, vinegar, sugar, mustard and salt to make a vinaigrette; season with pepper and whisk in the shallots.

4 Add the spinach, watercress, tomatoes and asparagus and gently toss to coat. Divide the salad between 4 plates, top with bacon pieces and shave Parmesan over the salad. Season with ground pepper and serve.

CARIBBEAN STYLE PORK

Ingredients

8 ripe tomatoes

½ ripe mango, pitted and finely chopped

3 tbsp mango juice

2 tbsp snipped chives

6 tbsp olive oil, divided

Hot red pepper sauce, to taste

Salt and freshly ground pepper, to taste

2 tbsp finely chopped basil leaves

1 tbsp finely chopped rosemary leaves

1 tbsp tomato paste (purée)

3 cloves garlic, finely chopped

4 (6-oz / 180 g) boneless pork chops

Method

Prep and cook time: 30 min

1 Fill a large bowl with ice water. Bring a large saucepan of water to a boil. One or two at a time, add the tomatoes and cook 8-10 seconds; quickly remove them with a slotted spoon to the ice water to cool. Repeat with the remaining tomatoes. Drain the tomatoes and slip off the skins. Halve and squeeze out the seeds; finely chop.

2 Combine the chopped tomatoes with the mango, mango juice, snipped chives, 2 tablespoons of the oil, hot pepper sauce, salt and plenty of pepper; set aside.

3 Pre heat the broiler (grill) to medium high. Heat the remaining 4 tablespoons oil in a skillet over medium heat; add the basil, rosemary, tomato paste (purée) and garlic. Cook, stirring, for 1 minute. Add the chops and turn once or twice so that both sides are coated in the tomato-herb mixture. Place the skillet under the broiler (grill). Cook, turning frequently, until juices run barely pink when pierced with a fork, about 10 minutes. Season with salt and plenty of pepper and serve at once with the tomato and mango sauce.

MEAT PATTIES WITH ONIONS AND TOMATOES

Ingredients

3 oz / 80 g white bread, crusts removed

1/3 cup / 80 ml milk

1 onion, finely chopped

1 tbsp butter

1¾ cups / 400 g mixed ground (minced) meat

2 eggs

1 tbsp hot mustard

1 chili, chopped

1 tsp dried marjoram

2 tbsp chopped fresh parsley

Breadcrumbs

Salt & freshly milled pepper

Oil, for brushing

4 tomatoes, quartered

2 red onions, cut into thick rings

Herbs, to garnish

Method

Prep and cook time: 30 min

1 For the meat patties, soak the bread in the milk. Heat the butter in a skillet and sauté the onion over a low heat until translucent.

2 Mix the ground meat with the soaked bread, eggs, mustard, chili, and onion. Add the marjoram and parsley and as many breadcrumbs as necessary to produce a shapeable mixture. Season with salt and pepper.

3 Shape into patties, brush with oil, and grill for 2–3 minutes each side. Sprinkle the red onions and tomatoes with a little oil and put on the grill with the patties.

4 Put the meat patties on plates with the tomatoes and onions. Garnish with herbs and serve with boiled new potatoes.

MOROCCAN CHICKEN WITH COUSCOUS

Ingredients

Around 2 lb / 1 kg chicken breast fillets

1 lemon

2 cloves garlic, finely chopped

4 tbsp olive oil

Salt & freshly milled pepper

2–3 tsp Moroccan spice mixture

For the yogurt dip:

1 cup / 250 ml whole-milk yogurt

Salt

1 pinch Moroccan spice mixture:
paprika, cumin, turmeric, ground
coriander, cayenne pepper and saffron

For the couscous:

1¼ cups / 250 g couscous

1 lemon

7 oz / 200 g ripe tomatoes, chopped

1 onion, finely chopped

1 small eggplant (aubergine), diced

1½ red bell peppers, deseeded and diced

1 tbsp olive oil

Freshly milled pepper

1 tbsp white wine vinegar

1 bunch cilantro (coriander)

Method

Prep and cook time: 50 min plus marinating time: 3 h

1 Remove any skin or fat from the meat. Cut the meat into 12 long thin strips. Wash the lemon, remove the zest with a zester and chop finely. Squeeze the lemon and reserve the juice.

2 Mix 2 tbsp lemon juice and 2 tbsp olive oil with the garlic, half of the lemon zest, salt, pepper, and the Moroccan spice mixture. Add the chicken, mix well, cover, and marinate in the refrigerator for about 3 hours.

3 Mix the yogurt and add the spices and salt to taste. Soak the wooden skewers in enough water to cover for 30 minutes (to prevent burning).

4 Cook the couscous according to the package instructions.

5 Squeeze the lemon and put the juice into a bowl. Add the vegetables to the lemon juice in the bowl.

6 Heat a little of the oil in a skillet, add the mixed vegetables and sauté until they are softened. Stir in the vinegar and mix the vegetables with the couscous along with the cilantro. Check the seasoning.

7 Preheat the broiler (grill). Thread the pieces of chicken on wooden skewers. Sprinkle the chicken with the rest of the oil and broil (grill) on all sides until the chicken in thoroughly cooked.

8 Spoon the couscous onto plates or into dishes, add chicken skewers and a little yogurt sauce to each and serve.

TURKEY AND PEACH KEBABS

Ingredients

1 lb 4 oz / 600 g skinless boneless turkey breast, cut into bite-size chunks

2 peaches, pitted and diced

1 red bell pepper, cut into bite-size pieces

Vegetable oil, for brushing

For the dip:

1 tbsp oil

1 small chili pepper, chopped (wear gloves to prevent irritation)

1 clove garlic, chopped

1 mango, pitted and finely chopped

1 tsp honey

Light soy sauce, to taste

Fish sauce, to taste

Sea salt, to taste

Hot red pepper flakes, to taste

Method

Prep and cook time: 30 min

1 Preheat the grill or broiler. Soak 8 wooden skewers in water to cover for at least 30 minutes (to prevent burning).

2 Thread the turkey, peaches and bell pepper pieces onto the skewers, alternating them as you go. Brush with oil and grill, turning frequently, 6-8 minutes, or until cooked through. Set aside and keep warm.

3 Meanwhile, to prepare the dip, heat the oil in a small skillet, add the chili and garlic and sauté briefly. Add the mango and honey and a little water; bring to a boil and cook, scraping browned bits from the skillet. Add soy sauce and fish sauce to taste and remove from the heat.

4 Put the turkey and peach skewers on plates, drizzle with a little of the dip and sprinkle with salt and pepper flakes. Serve the dip separately in small bowls.

HALIBUT
WITH MANGO
AND LIME SALSA

Ingredients

4 (5-6 oz / 150 g) halibut fillets

Salt and freshly ground pepper, to taste

Juice of 3 limes, divided

1 tbsp butter

2 ripe mangos, finely diced

4 tbsp mango juice

1 tsp brown sugar

1 pinch cayenne pepper

1 tbsp chopped cilantro (coriander);
reserve a few leaves to garnish

1 lime, thinly sliced, to garnish

1 lemon, thinly sliced, to garnish

Method

Prep and cook time: 30 min

1 Preheat the grill or broiler.

2 Season the fish with salt and pepper and sprinkle each with 1 tablespoon of the lime juice. Grill or broil the fish on both sides for 5-6 minutes.

3 Meanwhile, heat the butter in a skillet over medium heat and add the diced mango. Briefly sauté, then stir in the remaining lime juice and mango juice and season to taste with salt, brown sugar and cayenne. Add the cilantro (coriander).

4 Put the fish onto plates with the mango-lime sauce and serve garnished with slices of lime and lemon and cilantro leaves.

TOMATO SLICES WITH CAPERS AND LEMON ZEST

Ingredients

2 lb / 1 kg plum tomatoes

1 tsp sugar

Sea salt & freshly milled pepper

Olive oil

½ lemon

Some caper berries, to garnish

Method

Prep and cook time: 15 min

1 Chop the tomatoes into thick slices. Sprinkle sugar, salt, and freshly milled pepper over the top.

2 Wash the lemon, remove the zest with a zester and chop finely, and collect the juice in a cup.

3 Drizzle olive oil over the top. Place the tomatoes in a hot grill pan for about 1 minute each side. Remove and arrange onto plates. Drizzle lemon juice over the top, garnish with lemon zest and caper berries, and serve.

CHICKEN ON STIR-FRIED VEGETABLES

Ingredients

1–2 tsp Chinese five-spice powder

2 limes, zest and juice

12–14 tbsp dark soy sauce

4 chicken breast fillets

11 oz / 300 g snow peas (mangetout), trimmed

1 medium sized zucchini (courgette), sliced

7 oz / 200 g carrots, peeled and cut into matchsticks

2 tbsp oil

½ tsp chili powder

Salt

Scant ½ cup / 100 ml vegetable broth (stock)

3–4 oz / 75–100 g pea sprouts (or bean sprouts if unavailable)

2 tbsp sesame seeds (toasted)

Method

Prep and cook time: 40 min

1 Mix the five-spice powder, the zest and juice of the limes, and 6–8 tbsps. of the soy sauce to make a marinade; marinate the chicken for about 15 minutes.

2 Broil (grill) the chicken under a medium heat until cooked through, for 3–5 minutes on each side (depending on thickness).

3 Meanwhile, heat the oil in a wok. Add the snow peas (mangetout) and stir-fry for 1 minute. Add the zucchini (courgettes) and carrots and cook for a further 2 minutes. Add the chili powder, 2 tbsp soy sauce, and salt. Then add the broth (stock) and cook for a further 5 minutes.

4 Wash and drain the pea sprouts and add to the vegetables with the sesame seeds. Stir-fry for a further 2 minutes.

5 Slice the chicken and drizzle with the remaining soy sauce (or to taste). Serve the stir-fried vegetables onto plates and put the chicken on top.

MOROCCAN LAMB KEBABS WITH YOGURT SAUCE

Ingredients

1lb 12 oz / 800 g lamb, from the leg

3 oz/ 80 g mixed salad leaves

4 pita breads

1 lemon

8 wooden skewers

For the marinade:

Juice of 1 lemon

3–4 tbsp olive oil

2 sprigs rosemary, roughly chopped

½ inch / 1 cm fresh ginger, freshly grated

1 pinch cumin

1 chili pepper, finely chopped

For the yogurt sauce:

1 clove garlic

1 bunch parsley, roughly chopped

14 oz/ / 400 g natural yogurt

1 tsp lemon zest

Salt & white pepper

Method

Prep and cook time: 15 min plus Marinating time: 2 h

1 Mix all the marinade ingredients and put into a freezer bag.

2 Cut the meat into ¾ inch (2 cm) cubes and put into the freezer bag with the marinade. Seal and knead to make sure the meat is coated in the marinade. Put into the refrigerator and leave for at least 2 hours. Soak the wooden skewers in enough water to cover for 30 minutes (to prevent burning).

3 For the yogurt sauce, peel and press the garlic. Put into a bowl with the rest of the sauce ingredients and mix thoroughly. Season with salt and pepper. Chill in the refrigerator.

4 Heat the broiler (grill). Take the meat out of the marinade and thread on the wooden skewers. Broil (grill) on all sides for 5–7 minutes. Meanwhile, fold the pita breads and briefly toast/warm them. Cut the lemon into 8 wedges.

5 Arrange the kebabs on plates with the pita bread. Garnish with salad and sprinkle with yogurt sauce. The remaining sauce can be served separately.

APPLE AND CELERIAC SALAD

Ingredients

3 cups / 400–500 g celeriac

3–4 apples

3 tbsp lemon juice

2 sprigs parsley or celeriac leaves

1¼ cups / 300 g low-fat yogurt

Salt & pepper

1 pinch sugar

Brown bread, for serving

Method

Prep and cook time: 20 min

1 Peel the celeriac and cut into slices. Cook in boiling, salted water for about 3 minutes. Drain, place immediately into cold water, then drain again.

2 Peel and quarter the apples and remove the core. Cut into thin slices. Drizzle lemon juice over the apples. Cut the slices of celeriac into thin sticks and mix with the apples.

3 Chop the parsley (or celeriac leaves) into thin strips.

4 Season the yoghurt with salt, pepper, and a pinch of sugar, then add to the apple and celeriac and stir well. Season to taste with salt and pepper. Divide into bowls, sprinkle the parsley (or celeriac leaves) over the top and serve with a few slices of brown bread.

MEDITERRANEAN VEGETABLES

Ingredients

2 red bell peppers, cut in half lengthways and deseeded

4 tbsp olive oil

12 stalks asparagus

4 large tomatoes, cut into quarters

2 red onions, thickly sliced

Juice of 1 lemon

1 cup / 100 g black olives

Parmesan cheese shavings, to garnish

Method

Prep and cook time: 45 min

1 Heat the oven to 400ºF (200ºC / Gas Mark 6). Brush the bell peppers with a little oil, place on a cookie sheet and roast in the oven, skin side up, for 15 minutes or until the skin is charred.

2 Meanwhile, trim the asparagus and plunge into boiling salted water for 3 minutes. Drain, refresh in cold water and pat dry with kitchen paper.

3 Remove the bell peppers from the oven and turn the temperature down to 300ºF (150ºC / Gas Mark 2). Brush the tomato quarters with a little oil and place on a cookie sheet. Bake in the oven for 15 minutes.

4 Peel the skins away from the bell peppers, roughly chop the flesh and drizzle with a little oil.

5 Heat a griddle pan until very hot. Brush the onion slices with a little oil and cook in the griddle pan for 2 minutes on each side.

6 To serve, arrange the roast bell peppers, asparagus, tomatoes and onions onto plates. Drizzle over the remaining oil and the lemon juice, season with salt and pepper and garnish with the olives and shaved Parmesan cheese.

SPICY NOODLE SALAD

Ingredients

1 carrot

1 cucumber

2 shallots

½ cup /50 g bean sprouts

3 red chilis

7 oz / 200 g rice noodles

Cilantro (coriander) and mint leaves, shredded

For the Nuoc Cham Sauce:

5 cloves garlic, chopped very finely

5 red chilis, deseeded and chopped very finely

3½ tbsp Vietnamese fish sauce

Scant ½ cup / 100 ml water

3½ tbsp rice vinegar

¼ cup / 50 g sugar

Juice of 1 large lemon

Method

Prep and cook time: 25 min

1 Peel and halve the carrot and cucumber. Remove the cucumber seeds, cut the cucumber in half and cut lengthways into long, very thin strips. Cut the carrot into long very thin sticks. Peel the shallots and slice thinly. Wash and drain the bean sprouts. Halve and deseed the chilies and cut into rings. Reserve a couple of chili rings to garnish.

2 Cook the noodles in boiling, salted water for about 2 minutes. Then drain, refresh in cold water and drain thoroughly. Set aside.

3 For the sauce, put all the ingredients apart from the lemon juice into a pan and heat, but do not let it boil. Then remove from heat and let cool. Stir in the lemon juice when the sauce is cold.

4 Put the noodles, cucumber, carrots, shallots, chilies and 6 tbsp of Nuoc Cham sauce into a large bowl and mix. Serve on plates, sprinkled with herbs and the reserved chili rings.

GRILLED SHRIMP AND SCALLOP

Ingredients

4 large shrimp (or prawns), deveined and peeled

4 medium scallops

1 stalk lemongrass

4 tbsp olive oil

2 tbsp lemon juice

2 cloves garlic, minced

1 good pinch saffron threads, crumbled

Salt and freshly ground pepper

4 small red chilies

About 4 oz / 100 g cellophane noodles

2 tbsp vegetable oil

2 scallions (spring onions), thinly sliced on the diagonal

1–2 tbsp dry white wine

1 good pinch turmeric

1 head baby bok choy, quartered

Method

Prep and cook time: 40 min

1 Preheat the grill. Quarter the lemongrass stalk lengthwise and thread 1 shrimp (or prawn) and 1 scallop onto each piece.

2 In a small bowl, combine the olive oil, lemon juice, garlic and saffron threads; season with salt and pepper. Brush the skewers and the chilies with the marinade and grill, turning and brushing frequently with the marinade, 3-4 minutes.

3 Cook the noodles according to the package instructions; drain and set aside.

4 Meanwhile, heat the vegetable oil in a skillet and add the scallions (spring onions); sauté briefly. Add the wine and turmeric; bring to a boil, scraping up browned bits from the skillet, and cook until the scallions are glazed. Set aside and season with salt and pepper.

5 Place a bok choy piece on each of 4 plates. Add the noodles and sprinkle with scallions. Place a shrimp and scallop skewer and a chili on top and serve.

GRILLED PEARS WITH SWEET RICOTTA CREAM

Ingredients

2 pears

4 tbsp lemon juice, divided

½ cup / 100 g ricotta

4 tbsp honey, divided

Ground cinnamon, to garnish

Chocolate curls, to garnish

Mint leaves, to garnish

Method

Prep and cook time: 20 min

1 Preheat the grill or broiler.

2 Peel pears if desired; quarter and core. Brush with 2 tablespoons of the lemon juice and grill until browned, 2–3 minutes.

3 Meanwhile, in a small bowl, mix the ricotta with 2 tablespoons of the honey and the remaining lemon juice until smooth.

4 To serve, put two pear quarters on each plate, spoon a little ricotta over each and drizzle with the rest of the honey. Dust with cinnamon and scatter with chocolate curls and mint leaves.

GRILLED PEACHES
WITH AMARETTI
BUTTER

Ingredients

1 egg yolk

1/8 cup / 30 g sugar

1 good pinch ground cinnamon

Scant 1/2 cup /100 ml light cream

3–4 oz / 80–100 g amaretti cookies

1/2 stick / 50 g butter, softened

6 firm ripe peaches

1 tbsp sunflower oil

Method

Prep and cook time: 30 min, plus 3 h freezing time

1 Line a baking sheet or tray with foil or parchment.

2 In a large bowl, beat the egg yolk with the sugar for 10 minutes, until pale and creamy. Mix in the cinnamon.

3 In a separate bowl, whip the cream until stiff and fold into the mixture. Shape into 2-tablespoon portions and arrange on the prepared baking sheet; freeze until firm, about 3 hours.

4 Preheat the broiler (grill). Using 4 sheets of foil, shape small "bowls" large enough to hold three peach halves and brush each with a little oil.

5 Put the amaretti into a zip-close plastic bag; seal, squeezing out air. Crush to fine crumbs with a rolling pin. Then combine with the butter and rub together to form coarse crumbs.

6 Place three peach halves in each foil dish with the cut surface facing up; sprinkle with amaretti crumbs. Place on a baking sheet and broil (grill) until soft, about 5 minutes.

7 Put the peaches with their juices onto plates, add a portion of ice cream and drizzle with a little of the juice.

Published by Transatlantic Press

First published in 2010

Transatlantic Press
38 Copthorne Road, Croxley Green, Hertfordshire WD3 4AQ

© Transatlantic Press

Images and Recipes by StockFood © The Food Image Agency

Recipes selected by Jonnie Léger, StockFood

A catalogue record for this book is available from the British Library.

ISBN 978-1-908533-68-5

Printed in China